MW00440689

What Really Happened Christmas Morning?

Ralph O. Muncaster

HARVEST HOUSE PUBLISHERS
Eugene, Oregon 97402

Cover by Terry Dugan Design, Minneapolis, Minnesota

By Ralph O. Muncaster

Are There Hidden Codes in the Bible?
Can Archaeology Prove the New Testament?
Can Archaeology Prove the Old Testament?
Can You Trust the Bible?
Creation vs. Evolution
Creation vs. Evolution Video
Does the Bible Predict the Future?
How Do We Know Jesus Is God?
Is the Bible Really a Message from God?
Science—Was the Bible Ahead of Its Time?
What Is the Proof for the Resurrection?
What Really Happened Christmas Morning?
What Really Happens When You Die?

WHAT REALLY HAPPENED CHRISTMAS MORNING?
Copyright © 2000 by Ralph O. Muncaster
Published by Harvest House Publishers
Eugene, Oregon 97402

Library of Congress Cataloging-in-Publication Data

Muncaster, Ralph O.
    What really happened Christmas morning? / Ralph O. Muncaster.
        p. cm. — (Examine the evidence series)
    ISBN 0-7369-0323-2
        1. Jesus Christ—Nativity—Biblical teaching. 2. Bible—Evidences, authority, etc.
I. Title.

BT315.2.M855 2000
232.92—dc21   00-024158

00 01 02 03 04 05 06 07 08 09 / BP / 10 9 8 7 6 5 4 3 2 1

Contents

The First Christmas—
What If . . . ?

What if the biblical account of the first
Christmas is all true?

Then it's certainly a message of great joy for all who accept God's plan. . . for all who establish a relationship with Him.

The message of Christmas goes beyond the birth of an infant, beyond shepherds, a star, Bethlehem, and the magi. The basic message of Christmas deals with an age-old promise—a promise of God in human flesh—a promise of an eternal Savior. The first Christmas is just the prelude to the Bible's in-depth description of how to have a relationship with God forever. A relationship that promises an eternity of no more tears, no more death, no more pain, and unbelievable joy. The alternative, however, is a horror beyond description. Christmas involves both sides . . . a promise of good, and a promise of bad. And it provides a clear way for everyone to choose the promise of good.

So if the biblical account of Christmas is true, it
means everyone must choose his own destiny. . .
today and eternally. This makes the truth of
Christmas, without a doubt, the most important issue
for anyone to understand in his lifetime—more
important than the next vacation, more important
than the next golf game, and even more important
than the next paycheck.

Fortunately God has provided more evidence of the Christmas message than of any other event in human history. We don't need to accept it on blind faith. Even so, just as with the acceptance of any historical fact or religious belief, the ultimate decision to believe and to follow requires a final step of faith.

The First Christmas—The *Real* Issues

The baby born the first Christmas—Jesus Christ—has been analyzed far more than anyone in the history of the world.

Did Jesus Really Exist?

1.

The existence of Jesus is one of the best established facts in history.

Thousands of early manuscripts that survived major eradication attempts provide greater support for this than for any other accepted historical fact. And its confirmation by early Christian martyrs—alive at the time of Jesus— is undeniable

(see pages 10–15).

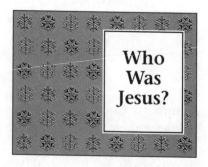

Who Was Jesus?

2.

Was Jesus just a man?
Just a great prophet?
Just a great teacher?

Evidence suggests otherwise. The miracles of Jesus were widely acknowledged—even by nonbelievers. Centuries-old prophecies provide "proof" of God's intervention. Even indirect archaeological evidence exists regarding the resurrection. And the disciples who knew the truth willingly, even joyfully, gave their lives to confirm what they knew. All this is compelling evidence (see pages 16–23, 38–43).

Why Does Jesus Matter?

3.

Joy on earth and forever.
Strength to face any challenge.
Eternal life with God.

Everyone must make a choice to accept or reject the baby born on the first Christmas. No decision is also a choice—of rejection. Jesus offers His free gifts to anyone (see pages 45–47).

The World at Jesus' Birth

The stage was perfectly set for
the first Christmas.

The World Situation

Political Stability—Never before or since has such a large percentage of the world lived at peace under a single government. The Roman Empire had expanded to include much of Europe, Africa, and Asia. About half of the world's 138 million people were governed by Rome. And the period of peace known as the *Pax Romana*, admired throughout history, lasted 200 years.

In 44 B.C. Julius Caesar was assassinated and his throne went to his great-grandnephew, Octavian, who was given the title Caesar Augustus. After defeating Mark Antony and Cleopatra, Augustus ruled from 27 B.C. to A.D. 14. Augustus began the great peace reforms and ordered a worldwide census (Luke 2:1), which historians believe may have been the census that brought Mary and Joseph to Bethlehem (see pages 36, 37—"When Was Jesus Born?").

Transportation—For the first time in history, an elaborate network of highways and sea routes made transportation throughout the empire relatively easy. This was vital to the rapid spread of Christianity.

Communication—The world was becoming unified as the level of education increased, and the language of *Koine* Greek (the dialect of the New Testament) was becoming common. As a result, it was easier and quicker to spread new ideas and thinking across a multicultural world than ever before.

Bethlehem, Nazareth, and Jerusalem

Jerusalem was the most prominent city in the Middle East. As well as being the political and religious center for the Jewish people, it was a regional seat of Roman government and was the residence of Herod.

Nazareth was on a major trade route from the ports of Tyre and Sidon, both known for vice and prostitution—as was Nazareth. The great city of Sepphoris, just four miles from Nazareth, was the capital of Galilee in Jesus' youth and was being rapidly expanded to honor its new leader, Herod Antipas. As carpenters, Joseph and Jesus almost certainly spent time there. (Excavation of Sepphoris is far from complete.)

Bethlehem of Judea was a small rural town, located a few miles south of Jerusalem. Even in Jesus' day, Bethlehem had significance as the burial place of Rachel (Jacob's wife), the place of the courtship of Ruth and Boaz, and the birthplace of King David.

Christmas—The Historical Record

The historical record regarding the birth of most great people is very limited. Consider John F. Kennedy or Julius Caesar—how much do we really know about either's birth? Relatively speaking, we know a lot about the first Christmas. The primary sources are Luke and Matthew within the Bible.

Luke

The credibility of Luke as a historian was verified by Sir William Ramsay, perhaps the world's greatest archaeologist, a skeptic who began extensive research to disprove Luke. His colleagues expected Ramsay to uncover evidence to disprove much of the New Testament once and for all. Yet Ramsay's final analysis surprised nearly everyone. After 30 years of study, Ramsay found Luke to be accurate in every detail. Ramsay even called Luke one of the "greatest historians of all time." Not surprisingly, Ramsay converted to Christianity.

How Evidence Was Collected

As with any biography, evidence was collected by Luke through interviews with people and study of records at the time (Luke 1:1-4). The importance of Luke's work *during the time of the eyewitnesses* is often overlooked.

Luke's (and Matthew's) information was collected and recorded during the lifetimes of those involved. Any time history is documented during the lifetime of those contemporary to the events, *it must stand the test of eyewitness critics*. Otherwise it will not be accepted and will vanish into obscurity. Today, if someone wrote that John F. Kennedy was born from a virgin and rose from the dead, it would *not* become a widely accepted historical record.

The events of Jesus' life were quite remarkable and certainly would have been extensively corroborated by many witnesses. If there had not been exceptional agreement among eyewitnesses about the events—including the virgin birth, the miracles, and the resurrection, undoubtedly the historical record would have quickly vanished. Instead it became, by far, the most recorded account ever.

"People Talked"

Founders of other religions have claimed divine insight from *solitary* encounters with angels or gods—easy claims to fabricate. In contrast, the Bible indicates *many people* saw and discussed the extraordinary events:

Who?	Which event did they see and discuss?
All living in "the hill country of Judea"	Zechariah's loss and regaining of speech (Luke 1:21,22; 1:65,66)
Neighbors and relatives	Elizabeth's miracle child (Luke 1:58)
Shepherds and others	The coming of the angels and the birth of Jesus (Luke 2:15-20)
Herod and "all Jerusalem"	Jesus' birth and the coming of the magi (Matthew 2:1-3)
More than 500 people	The resurrection of Jesus (1 Corinthians 15:6,7)

The Christmas Witnesses

Consider again John F. Kennedy, Julius Caesar, or any such historical figure. Why do we have so little eyewitness testimony about their births? Perhaps it's because nothing really startling happened. But Jesus' birth was different. The events were *memorable*. And there were *many* witnesses, so events could easily be verified later during Luke's investigation.

Consider the Shepherds

What would have prompted low-status shepherds to widely proclaim the "amazing events" if they hadn't been true? Other people would probably have thought that a miraculous appearance of angels, followed by the prophesied discovery of Jesus, was strange or untrue. And after all, Bethlehem was a small town. When Luke wrote about the events later, they could easily have been corroborated by eyewitnesses (Luke 2:17,18).

Consider Simeon and Anna

These were two well-known, highly esteemed people. Both proclaimed the infant Jesus to be the long-awaited Messiah—a powerful and daring statement to be made by such respected individuals. Perhaps at the time the proclamations were simply acknowledged in passing. Later they became highly significant. Again, others were eyewitnesses to these statements (Luke 2:25-38).

Other Unforgettable Events

Herod's slaughter of innocent children would not have been forgotten by local people recounting the events of the first Christmas. Even the visit by the magi (the "wise men") would have been unforgettable. The magi were men of importance who would have arrived with much fanfare (see pages 34, 35).

Consider Zechariah and Elizabeth

It would have been a very serious offense for Zechariah to invent a vision of angels—a vision that came during holy ceremonies—or to give false prophecy. Yet Zechariah indicated to the other priests that his barren wife, Elizabeth, would bear a son. With no ultrasound in those days, and given that Elizabeth was well past childbearing age, such statements would have been very costly to him if untrue. However, Zechariah's loss and regaining of the ability to speak, as foretold by the angel, added weight to the prophecy. Again, eyewitnesses were present who would have recalled such events (Luke 1:5-66).

Consider All the Witnesses to Statements of Jesus' Deity

Jesus' deity was proclaimed at His birth and later verified by His death and resurrection. His deity was proclaimed *before birth* by angels, by Elizabeth and Zechariah (Luke 1:43), and by Mary. It was proclaimed *at birth* by angels who were witnessed by shepherds. And it was proclaimed *soon after birth* by Simeon and Anna. His deity was foretold in scores of prophecies and was later confirmed by His resurrection from death—and His appearance to hundreds of witnesses (1 Corinthians 15:6).

Manuscript Evidence
of Jesus' Birth

Although evidence shows that Luke's original history was accurately recorded during the time of eyewitnesses to the events, how do we know Luke's account was not changed over time? The answer is in the explosion of copies of the recorded evidence *within a very short time of the actual events*. Today, we have in existence *many more* early manuscripts about Jesus than for *any other event up to that period*—events which are nonetheless widely accepted as fact.

Comparison to Historical Manuscripts[1]

Julius Caesar's great campaigns in France have been taught as historical fact for centuries. The source of this history is Caesar's *Gallic Wars*, written in the first century B.C. How does such a prominent source compare in documentary evidence to the accounts of the first Christmas? *It's not even in the same league.* In fact, no other event of antiquity even comes close in documentary evidence to the life of Jesus. We have in existence today more than 24,000 early manuscripts of the New Testament, compared to only 10 of the Gallic Wars. Copies exist that were written within 25 years of Jesus' time—versus 1000 years from the events for the earliest copies of *Gallic Wars*.

Ancient Works	Number of Existing Early Manuscripts	Elapsed Time from Event to Earliest Existing Manuscript
Gallic Wars—Julius Caesar	10	1000 years
History—Pliny the Younger	7	750 years
History—Thucydides	8	1300 years
History—Herodotus	8	1300 years

Ancient Works	Number of Existing Early Manuscripts	Elapsed Time from Event to Earliest Existing Manuscript
Works of Sophocles	193	1400 years
Works of Euripides	9	1500 years
Works of Aristotle	49	1400 years
Works of Aristophanes	10	1200 years
The New Testament	**24,000 +**	**25 years**

Attempts to Eradicate Evidence

The number of existing early documents of the New Testament would be incredible enough if times had been "normal" during that period. However, in the first three centuries a number of opponents to the New Testament and Christianity attempted to eradicate them. Why? Because Christianity was a threat to many peoples' livelihood. Religious leaders and many merchants had to choose between making money and tolerating or accepting Christianity. For instance, the sale of idols plummeted, causing some people to request the execution of Christians (see page 17). And of course some early Jews also attempted to stop the spread of Christianity through persecution.

Nero and later Roman Emperors increased persecution substantially. And in A.D. 303 an edict was issued to destroy all Bibles. Anyone caught with a Bible was condemned to death.

Non-Christian Evidence of Jesus

Very few written works of *anything* exist from the period of A.D. 30 to A.D. 60. All existing works from A.D. 50 to A.D. 70 are said to fit between bookends only a foot apart.[1] In the years close to and after Nero's killing of Christians in A.D. 64, we find the following references to Jesus and his followers:

Thallus (circa A.D. 52)—Historical work referenced by Julius Africanus explains the darkness at the time of Christ's death as a solar eclipse. While an eclipse did not occur in that period (pointed out by Julius Africanus), reference to Jesus' death was stated as a matter of fact.

Josephus (circa A.D. 64–93)—This Jewish historian referred to Jesus, His miracles, His crucifixion, and His disciples. Also referenced are James, "brother of Jesus who was called the Christ," and John the Baptist.

Cornelius Tacitus (A.D. 64–116)—Writing to dispel rumors that Nero caused the great fire of Rome in A.D. 64, he refers to Christians as the followers of "Christus," who "had undergone the death penalty in the reign of Tiberius, by sentence of the procurator

Writings from Jewish Rabbis (circa A.D. 40–180)

Several passages from the *Talmud* and other Jewish writings clearly refer to Jesus Christ. References include:

- The "hanging" (on a cross) of Jesus on the eve of Passover.

- Identifying Jesus and the names of five of His disciples.

- Healing in the name of Jesus.

- Scoffing at the "claim" of Jesus' virgin birth and implying His "illegitimacy."

Pontius Pilatus." The resurrection was called "the pernicious superstition."

Pliny the Younger (circa A.D. 112)—As governor of Bithynia in Asia Minor, he requested guidance from Rome regarding the proper test to give Christians before executing them. (If they renounced the faith, cursed Jesus, and worshiped the statue of emperor Trajan, they were set free.)

Hadrian (circa A.D. 117–138)—In response to questions regarding the punishment of Christians who drew people away from pagan gods, which affected the sale of idols, Hadrian commanded that they be "examined" regarding their faith (similar to the response to Pliny the Younger).

Suetonius (circa A.D. 120)—A historian wrote about events in the late 40s–60s. He referred to Christ, the "mischievous and novel superstition" of the resurrection, and to Christians being put to death by Nero.

Phlegon (circa A.D. 140)—Referenced by Julius Africanus and Origen, he referred to the "eclipse," the earthquake, and to Jesus' prophecies.

Lucian of Samosata (circa A.D. 170)—This Greek satirist wrote about Christians, Christ, the crucifixion, Christian martyrs, and "novel beliefs."

Mara Bar-Serapion (before A.D. 200)—A Syrian philosopher, he wrote from prison to his son, comparing Jesus to Socrates and Plato.

Archaeological Evidence About Jesus

Archaeologists have discovered substantial support for many details of Jesus' life (see *Can Archaeology Prove the New Testament?* in the *Examine the Evidence* series). Some examples include:

Jesus' Birthplace[2]

To us, a "stable" is a type of wooden barn outside a home. In Jesus' day, stables were often within courtyards of homes or in caves outside. The actual site believed to be the stable of Jesus' birth was identified relatively shortly after His resurrection. Early authors (Jerome and Paulinus of Nola) indicate the site was "marked" about the time of Hadrian (circa A.D. 120), and archaeologists have never seriously disputed it. The site is a cave located beneath the Church of the Nativity in Bethlehem.

Indirect Evidence of the Resurrection[3]

Evidence that the people of Jesus' time believed in the resurrection has been found on bone caskets (ossuaries) that were discovered in a sealed tomb outside Jerusalem in 1945. Coins minted in about A.D. 50 were found inside the caskets, dating the burial to within about 20 years of Jesus' crucifixion. Markings in the caskets are clearly legible and include the words (in Greek): "Jesus, help" and "Jesus, let him arise." The caskets also contain several crosses, clearly marked in charcoal. This is powerful evidence that early Christians believed in Jesus' ability to triumph over death.

Prior to the resurrection, "grave robbing" was not considered a serious offense. The resurrection changed that. An inscription found on a tomb in Nazareth warns that anyone found stealing from the tombs would receive the death penalty. Scholars believe the inscription was written as early as the reign of Tiberius (ended A.D. 37) or as late as the reign of Claudius (A.D. 41–54). In either case, it would have been shortly after the crucifixion. Naturally, Jesus' hometown of Nazareth would be of obvious "interest" to officials.

Jesus' Burial Shroud?

A burial shroud (the Shroud of Turin) is considered by many people to be the actual burial shroud of Jesus (Matthew 27:59; Mark 15:46; Luke 23:53). Several items support its authenticity:

1. Tests that confirm fiber type and small particles of limestone dust unique to the region.

2. Confirmation of blood from wounds positioned precisely as indicated in the accounts of Jesus' unique execution.

3. Confirmation of crucifixion as the likely cause of death.

4. Coins on eyes dated to about the time of the crucifixion.

Some experts have been able to mimic creation of the shroud's image using today's technology. Some believe the shroud to be a complex fourteenth-century hoax. The ultimate issue of its use by Jesus, however, will never be certain.

Prophecy—The "Proof" of Christmas

Although history can never be "proven," enormous statistical probability is often viewed as "proof" by scientists and mathematicians. God's involvement in the life of Jesus is statistically certain.

The prophecies contained in the Old Testament were written long before Jesus' birth. The famous Dead Sea scrolls provide irrefutable evidence that they were not tampered with over the centuries. Of the 469 prophecies contained in the Old Testament, 467 have been verified as fulfilled (we have no record of the fulfillment of the other two). Perhaps the most fascinating of these prophecies are the ones regarding Jesus.

Prophecies About Jesus

Who

Jesus' ancestors were prophesied:

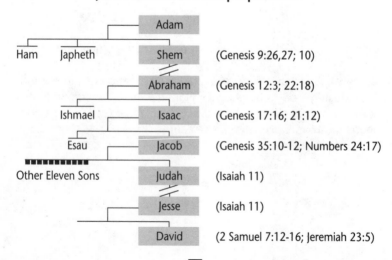

Adam	
Ham Japheth Shem	(Genesis 9:26,27; 10)
Abraham	(Genesis 12:3; 22:18)
Ishmael Isaac	(Genesis 17:16; 21:12)
Esau Jacob	(Genesis 35:10-12; Numbers 24:17)
Other Eleven Sons Judah	(Isaiah 11)
Jesse	(Isaiah 11)
David	(2 Samuel 7:12-16; Jeremiah 23:5)

What

The life and role of Jesus also were precisely recorded in prophecies written down hundreds of years before His birth. The descriptions of what Jesus would become include predictions of the miraculous elements of His birth, His divine nature, and details of His earthly life. The Scriptures prophesied that:

1. A virgin would be with child (Isaiah 7:14).

2. The child would be God, not a normal human being. The name Immanuel literally means "God with us" (Isaiah 7:14).

3. The One who was born would be an eternal Savior (Isaiah 9:6,7).

4. The Savior would be for both the Jews and the Gentiles (Isaiah 49:6).

5. He would work many miracles, including making the deaf hear, the blind see, the lame walk, and the mute speak (Isaiah 29:18; 35:5,6).

6. He would suffer greatly (Isaiah 53).

7. He would be crucified for human transgressions (Isaiah 53:5).

8. He would bear the sin of many and be made an intercessor (Isaiah 53:12).

9. He would be rejected by His own people, the Jews (Isaiah 53:3; Psalm 118:22; Matthew 21:42-46)

When

Prophecy of the Date of Palm Sunday

Although complex until understood, this prophecy, which Daniel recorded about 535 B.C., predicted Jesus' final entry into Jerusalem to the day (Daniel 9:20-27). The prophecy has been called:

Daniel's "Seventy Sevens"

- Sixty-nine periods of 7 (years) will pass from the decree to rebuild Jerusalem until the coming of the "Anointed One" ("Messiah" in Hebrew). This dates Jesus' entry into Jerusalem on Palm Sunday.

- After that time the Anointed One will be cut off (Hebrew *yikaret*, meaning a sudden, violent end—such as crucifixion).

- And following that time, the city and the temple will be destroyed.

> Daniel, a Hebrew, received the prophetic revelation in 535 B.C. Using the Hebrew definition of year (360 days), we find: 69 x 7 years = 173,880 days.

The actual decree to rebuild Jerusalem was given by Artaxerxes[4] on March 14, 445 B.C. (the first day of Nisan that year—see Nehemiah 2:1-6).

Using the actual 365-day calendar along with adjustments for leap years, and the final scientific adjustment (leap year dropped every 128 years), we find this number of days brings us precisely to:[5]

April 6, A.D. 32

Fulfillment in History: Jesus' ministry began in the fifteenth year of Tiberius Caesar (Luke 3:1), whose reign began in A.D. 14. A chronological analysis of Jesus' ministry shows three years leading up to the final week, in A.D. 32.

The Royal Observatory in Greenwich, England, confirms the Sunday before Passover that year to be:

April 6, A.D. 32

22

Other prophecy elements were fulfilled as well:

- Jesus was crucified 3½ days later.
- The Romans destroyed the city and the temple in A.D. 70.

Where

Precise City of Jesus' birth

The Bible specified that Jesus would be born in Bethlehem, in Ephrathah (that is, in Judea—there was another Bethlehem closer to Joseph's home in Nazareth—see Micah 5:2).

Other Prophecies About Jesus

- He is King, rides on a donkey (Zechariah 9:9)

- Suffers, is rejected (Isaiah 53:1-3)

- Is crucified, pierced (Psalm 22:16)

- Lots are cast for His clothing (Psalm 22:18)

- No bones broken (Psalm 34:19,20)

- Given gall and wine (Psalm 69:20-22)

- Pierced with a spear (Zechariah 12:10)

- Posterity to serve Him (Psalm 22:30)

- Betrayed by a friend (Psalm 41:9)

- For 30 pieces of silver (Zechariah 11:12,13)

- The silver is cast on the temple floor, then used to buy a potter's field (Zechariah 11:13)

> Experts in statistics estimate the probability of all these prophecies coming true in ANY one man is about one chance in 10^{99}—less than the odds of correctly selecting one electron out of all the matter in the universe—or essentially zero *without divine intervention.*[1]

The First Christmas—

1.
The Prophecies

Detailed prophecies foretold many facts about the Messiah (see pages 20–23):
Who He would be,
What He would do,
When He would come,
Where He would be born.

2.
The Star

A bright star appeared that triggered the visit of magi from the East (see page 44).

12.
Archaeology

Archaeologists believe they have located the site of Jesus' birth. Other compelling evidence of the existence of Jesus has also been discovered, as well as convincing proofs of widespread knowledge of the resurrection and the impact it made on people (see pages 18,19).

11.
The Jewish Record

Even those violently opposed to Jesus provide historical evidence of His existence, including indisputable references to prophecy and references in writings such as the *Talmud* (see pages 16,17).

10.
The Disciples' Martyrdom

Eleven people who certainly knew the truth about Jesus and the resurrection willingly—even joyfully—died to support the historical account. These deaths were not the result of random slaughter, but because of the purposeful effort of these disciples to ensure that the historical record remained intact—at the cost of their eventual execution (see pages 38,39).

9.
Historical Martyrs

Millions of people, many of whom had been able to communicate with eyewitnesses, willingly died to preserve the historical record (see page 39).

Key Historical Issues

3.
The Christmas Witnesses

Many people saw the unusual events of the first Christmas and could corroborate the account widely circulated at the time. Only an accurate record could have survived such scrutiny (see pages 12,13).

4.
Herod's Slaughter of Children

An insecure tyrant, Herod decreed the slaughter of all male children under two years old in the area. Estimates suggest about 60 children were murdered (see page 35).

5.
The Magi

These powerful visitors came from the East. They knew about the coming Messiah from the teaching of Daniel, who was leader of the magi during the Jewish Exile. Herod was compelled to meet these important visitors (who are today the subject of many myths—see pages 34, 35).

6.
Paul's Change

A prominent leader in the persecution of Christians, Paul gave up wealth, position, and status once he encountered the risen Jesus. Paul recorded much of the New Testament (see page 40).

8.
The Manuscript Explosion

Never before or since has such an explosion of records of an event ever occurred as with the birth, life, and death of Jesus. The written historical record was available to many thousands of eyewitnesses (see pages 14,15).

7.
Rapid Church Formation

The events of Jesus' life caused the formation of the church—a body that survived the most focused and intensive persecution of all time (see page 15).

The Ancestors of Jesus
Before David

Genealogies were especially important to the Hebrews. Ancestry played a vital role in many legal rights. Only men (fathers) were included in official genealogies since few rights were given to women. Examination of the ancestry of Jesus provides many insights. In fact, Jesus descended from a wide variety of people, including a prostitute, murderers, adulterers, blasphemers, and even children born from incest. This should give everyone hope, regardless of his or her ancestral background.

Abraham is a pivotal person in history. He is considered both the father of the Jews (through Isaac, according to the Old Testament) and of the Arabs (through Ishmael, according to the Old Testament and the Qur'an).

From Adam to Noah to Abraham (Genesis 5)

At least one scholar has concluded that the line of descent from Adam to Noah contains a veiled prophecy of a Savior to come (though not all scholars agree with this conclusion). The *root* meanings of the names are:

Man • Appointed • Mortal • Sorrow • The Blessed God • Shall come down • Teaching • His Death shall bring • The despairing • Comfort.[6]

Adam	Man	Jared	Shall come down
Seth	Appointed	Enoch	Teaching
Enosh	Mortal	Methuselah	His death will bring
Kenan	Sorrow	Lamech	The despairing
Mahalalel	The Blessed God	Noah	Comfort

Luke, a doctor, provides the natural genealogy of Jesus from Adam to Mary.

Matthew, a tax collector writing primarily to the Jews, starts with Abraham and provides the official "legal" line through the "husband of Mary"—Joseph.

Shem to Abraham (Luke)

Genesis 5:32; 10:21	Shem
Genesis 10:22; 11:10	Arphaxad
Genesis 10:24	Shelah
Genesis 10:24	Eber
Genesis 11:16	Peleg
Genesis 11:18	Reu
Genesis 11:20	Serug
Genesis 11:22	Nahor
Genesis 11:24	Terah
Genesis 11:27; 17:5	Abraham

Isaac to David (Luke and Matthew)

Genesis 17:19; 21:3	Isaac
Genesis 25:26; 27:36	Jacob ("Israel")
Genesis 29:35; 46:12	Judah
Genesis 38:29; Ruth 4:12	Perez
Genesis 46:12; Ruth 4:18	Hezron
Ruth 4:19; 1 Chronicles 2:9	Ram
Numbers 1:7; 2:3; Ruth 4:19	Amminadab
Numbers 1:7; 2:3; Ruth 4:20	Nahshon
Ruth 4:20; 1 Chronicles 2:11	Salmon
Ruth 2:1; 4:21; Matthew 1:5	Boaz (wife: Ruth)
Ruth 4:17,21	Obed
Ruth 4:17,21; 1 Samuel 16:1	Jesse
Ruth 4:17,22; 1 Samuel 16:13	David

Tamar—Tricked her father-in-law Judah into thinking she was a prostitute (by hiding behind a veil) to enable their sexual relations to produce a child and heir. Tamar produced twins: Pharez (Perez) became an ancestor of Christ (Genesis 38:1-30).

Ruth—The gentile bride of Boaz. She became a prophetic model of the Church with Boaz being a "type" of Christ the Redeemer.[7]

Perez to **David**—Jewish law required that ten generations pass before any heir born through incest could have certain rights—including becoming king (Deuteronomy 23:2). This is why Saul (from the tribe of Benjamin) became the first king of Israel even though prophecy had already indicated the king would come from the line of Judah (Genesis 49:10).

The Ancestors of Jesus After David

David

Luke Reference	Mary's Line (Luke 3)	Matthew Reference	Joseph's Line (Matthew 1)
2 Samuel 5:14	Nathan	2 Samuel 12:24,25; 1 Chronicles 3:5; 14:4; 23:1; 2 Chronicles 1:12; 1 Kings 11:1	Solomon
Luke 3:31	Mattatha	1 Kings 11:43; 14:21; 2 Chronicles 12:13	Rehoboam
Luke 3:31	Menna	1 Kings 14:31; 2 Chronicles 11:20; 13:21	Abijah
Luke 3:31	Melea	1 Kings 15:8-24; 2 Chronicles 15:17; 16:12	Asa
Luke 3:30	Eliakim	1 Kings 15:24; 22:41-50; 2 Chronicles 20:35-37	Jehoshaphat
Luke 3:30	Jonam	1 Kings 22:50; 2 Kings 8:16; 2 Chronicles 21:14-20	Jehoram
Luke 3:30	Joseph	2 Kings 8:24-29; 2 Chronicles 22:9	Ahaziah
Luke 3:30	Judah	2 Kings 11:21; 12:1; 13:1	Joash
Luke 3:30	Simeon	2 Kings 12:21; 14:13	Amaziah
Luke 3:29	Levi	2 Kings 14:21; 15:1-27	Uzziah
Luke 3:29	Matthat	2 Kings 15:5,30	Jotham
Luke 3:29	Jorim	Isaiah 7:1	
Luke 3:29	Eliezer	2 Kings 15:38; Isaiah 7:1	Ahaz
Luke 3:29	Joshua	2 Kings 18:1; 1 Chronicles 3:13; Isaiah 37	Hezekiah
Luke 3:28	Er	2 Kings 21:1; 1 Chronicles 3:13	Manasseh
Luke 3:28	Elmadam	2 Kings 21:19; 1 Chronicles 3:14	Amon
Luke 3:28	Cosam	1 Kings 13:2; 2 Kings 21:24	Josiah
Luke 3:28	Addi	2 Kings 23:34; 24:1-7; Jeremiah 1:3,25; 2 Chronicles 36:4	Jehoiakim
Luke 3:28	Melki	2 Kings 24:6; 25:7; 2 Chronicles 36:8; Jeremiah 22:24	Jehoiachin
Luke 3:27	Neri	1 Chronicles 3:17; Ezra 3:2,8; Nehemiah 12:1	Shealtiel
Luke 3:27	Shealtiel	Haggai 1:1,12,14; 2:2	Zerubbabel
Luke 3:27	Zerubbabel	Matthew 1:13	Abiud
Luke 3:27	Rhesa	Matthew 1:13	Eliakim
Luke 3:27	Joanan	Matthew 1:13	Azor
Luke 3:26	Joda	Matthew 1:14	Zadok
Luke 3:26	Josech	Matthew 1:14	Akim
Luke 3:26	Semein	Matthew 1:14	Eliud
Luke 3:26	Mattathias	Matthew 1:15	Eleazar
Luke 3:26	Maath	Matthew 1:15	Matthan
Luke 3:25	Naggai	Matthew 1:16	Jacob
Luke 3:25	Esli		Joseph (Mary's husband)
Luke 3:25	Nahum		
Luke 3:25	Amos		
Luke 3:25	Mattathias		
Luke 3:24	Joseph		
Luke 3:24	Jannai		
Luke 3:24	Melki		
Luke 3:24	Levi		
Luke 3:24	Matthat		
Luke 3:23	Heli		

Joseph
(son-in-law)

Mary
(Luke 3)

Joseph
(Matthew 1)

Solomon—David's second son with Bathsheba. Their first died after David's sins of murder and adultery (2 Samuel 11). Overall, Solomon was a wise, good king (he built the Temple)—yet he had problems later in his reign.

After David, Mary's line came through David's son Nathan, whereas Joseph's line came through David's son Solomon.

Rehoboam—Solomon's son and heir to the throne became ruler of only two of the tribes of Israel (in Judah). As prophesied in Solomon's reign, the northern tribes broke away under separate leadership.

Hezekiah—A good king who "reopened the doors of the Temple." He also built a tunnel to provide drinking water to the city of Jerusalem. It can be seen today. Inscriptions date it to the time of Hezekiah's reign.

Manasseh—After becoming king at age 12, he was an evil king who built places of idol worship demolished by his predecessor, Hezekiah. He later repented.

Jehoiachin—An evil king—he was cursed by God and told that his family line would never inherit the throne of David—a seeming contradiction to prophecy about the line of Jesus (Jeremiah 22:24-30).

Because the genetic line of Jesus went through Mary, and only the *legal* line through Joseph, both the curse and the promise of Jesus as king remained valid.

The Journey to Bethlehem

A hundred-mile journey is taken for granted today—it's a very short plane ride. But imagine it thousands of years ago with no car, over rugged terrain. "A hundred miles" takes on a very different meaning.

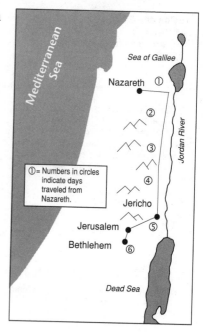

①= Numbers in circles indicate days traveled from Nazareth.

For starters, consider walking. Suddenly it's a major trek. Next add steep hills and valleys. The difficulty increases. Finally, consider a pregnant, near-term wife, with no doctors available. A casual journey becomes a major undertaking with considerable risk.

Joseph and Mary had to journey from Nazareth (population: about 200 families) to Bethlehem Ephrathah to register for a census. (There was another Bethlehem near Nazareth.) The trip would have taken about six days (Luke 2:1-5).

Day one would have been a journey east toward the southern end of the Sea of Galilee. Although a small amount of time might have been saved by going directly south through Samaria, it was common for Jews to avoid the land (Samaritans were disdained by the Jews).

The next day, a 60-mile trek down the River Jordan would begin. At least two nights would have to be spent en route before the travelers arrived at Jericho.

On day four or five, Joseph and Mary would have to make a rugged journey over the very treacherous terrain of the Judean wilderness. This land was filled with mountain lions, vipers, scorpions, and bandits. It would have been an exhausting ordeal.

Finally Jerusalem, the highlight of the journey, would be reached. Presumably, Joseph and Mary would at least visit the temple. After a ceremonial washing, they would offer a sacrifice of two turtledoves before heading southeast to Bethlehem.

The trip to Bethlehem from Jerusalem was short—about five miles. Because of the required census, it would be bustling with out-of-towners, the reason why there would be no room at the inns of the area. That night, after an exhausting journey, with no hospital, no doctors—only the smell and noise of a stable—the God of the universe would come to earth in a *completely dependent human form*. What an incredible and humble way to arrive!

The Night of Jesus' Birth

It probably started as a very ordinary night for the people of Bethlehem. It is only after the fact we can see that extraordinary events were taking place and wonder why there wasn't room at the inn or why there were no crowds.

To keep things in perspective, we need to understand the world at that time. There was no CNN late night news. There were no newspapers—not even much writing at all. There were no phones. Travel was very limited. Joseph and Mary—100 miles from home—might as well have been thousands of miles away. They had no communication whatsoever with their home town.

Mary had spent the past nine months under incredible duress from a unique pregnancy. Because of the situation, it would have been very unusual for Mary's family to broadcast her condition to other towns and villages. Presumably, they kept it quiet. (Joseph had even planned to "quietly divorce" Mary until an angel intervened—see Matthew 1:19.)

The Inn and Stable

The "inn" mentioned in the Bible (Greek *kataluma*) could have been a major structure, a house, or simply a shelter. The *caravanserais* (Eastern-style inns) common at the time were large buildings (about 100 yards on each side) formed around a large central courtyard where animals were kept. In such a case Jesus would have been born in the central courtyard on a ledge that served as the feeding area (or manger). More likely He was born in a cave (caves were commonly used as stables)—such as the site celebrated as the birthplace of Jesus in Bethlehem today (see page 18).

The Angel Gabriel

One of the assignments of angels was that of foretelling great news, as Gabriel did regarding the births of John the Baptist (Luke 1:19) and Jesus (Luke 1:26). The only other mention of Gabriel is in the book of Daniel, when Gabriel prophesies Jesus' entry into Jerusalem to become the ultimate sacrifice for mankind (see page 22). Thus, Gabriel foretold both the birth of the Savior and the rebirth of mankind.

Angels Singing in the Bible?

Songs of angels often seem synonymous with Christmas. However, only *twice* does the Bible mention angels singing: once at creation, before the fall of mankind (Job 38:7), and once at the end of time (Revelation 5:11,12), after the curse is removed.

A Solitary Birth

It was common in Jesus' time to use midwives in childbirth. Almost never was a birth undertaken alone, and it would have been unusual to have a pregnant woman rejected at an inn. Yet the Biblical account seems to indicate that Mary was virtually on her own at the birth (Luke 2:7 states "she" wrapped the baby in swaddling cloths and placed him in a manger—things typically done by a midwife). Mary was only a teenager or a woman in her early twenties at the time.

The Magi

The account of the visit of the magi (traditionally, "wise men") at first seems simply to be a colorful story emphasizing the mystery of the birth of Jesus. In reality, the magi, who probably came from Persia, played a very important part in the politics of the region at that time.

During the years preceding the birth of Jesus, there were numerous struggles between Rome and Persia. Palestine was essentially a "buffer state." Herod was granted the title "King of the Jews" three full years before he was able to occupy his own capital city (he had previously been driven out by the Persians).

Hence, Herod (a half Jew) was extremely insecure in his role. Furthermore, "full" Jews looked down on Herod. So the potential existed for Herod to be attacked from many directions, including through potential collusion between the Jews and Persians.

Add to this the fact that the ruler of Persia was aging and in ill health. The magi were given great power in Persia and often played key roles in governmental affairs. Their duties included selecting the kings of Persia. Hence, circumstances were in place that would certainly have "greatly troubled" the insecure Herod and the people of Jerusalem when the magi arrived (Matthew 2:3). In summary, we have:

- An insecure king (Herod, who killed even his own family members)

- A history of conflict with Persia

- A volatile situation with the ruler of Persia (he was old and ill)

- Powerful "kingmakers" (the magi) visiting Herod

- The magi seeking the "King of the Jews" (a title Herod himself held)

It's no surprise the magi got an audience with Herod, who was concerned that regional disputes could launch a new major conflict. The magi arrived with great pomp and ceremony. Despite the myths of "three kings" on camels, the magi would have ridden in on horses, complete with their own army. And the magi were not "kings." Herod even tolerated an obvious insult—that they were seeking a baby whom they called "King of the Jews" (Herod had that title). Not unlike a ruler of our time, Herod honored their presence, then proceeded with his own plan—killing all male babies in the area that might be a threat to him.

How the Magi Knew

How did the magi know to come to Palestine at that very time in search of the new king? The answer lies in the book of the prophet Daniel, who was appointed chief over the magi during the Jewish exile (Daniel 5:11). Daniel was given the prophecy which foretold precisely when the Messiah would enter Jerusalem as king (see page 22). The magi would also have known of the prophecy of a sign (a star) to indicate the coming Messiah. For some reason, however, the prophecy about the Messiah's birth taking place in Bethlehem (Micah 5:2) had not yet been fully recognized by the magi.

When Was Jesus Born?

The most widely referenced date of all time is the date of Jesus' birth. The calendar of our day uses that date as a reference for any year *B.C.* (Before Christ) or *A.D.* (Latin *Anno Domini*, the year of the Lord).Yet it's probably wrong. In A.D. 532, a monk named Dionysius Exiguus estimated the year of Jesus' birth. Evidence exists that suggests Exiguus misestimated by as many as seven years.

4 B.C. ?

The most commonly assumed (actual) date of Jesus' birth is 4 B.C. The basis for this view is a reference by the Jewish historian Josephus to an eclipse "shortly before" Herod the Great's death. (The presumed eclipse occurred on March 13, 4 B.C.[8]—although another eclipse occurred in 1 B.C.) Herod was alive at the time of Jesus' birth (Matthew 2). Using that information, 4 B.C. would be the closest possible year to the original estimate. Many Biblical resources suggest this date.

7 B.C. ?

A date of 7 B.C. for the appearance of the star of Bethlehem has been proposed, based on astronomical observations of Johannes Kepler (along with several alternative possibilities). This timing is supported by information about Roman censuses (which would have occurred about 7 or 8 B.C.). However, some scholars suggest other censuses were taken as well, and argue there is no firm evidence which census, and what local timing, actually brought Joseph and Mary to Bethlehem. Since alternative dates exist for both the appearance of the star and the census, there is no certainty that 7 B.C. is correct.

2 B.C. ?

The most exhaustive evidence may support a date of 2 B.C.[8]
Several sources seem to corroborate the date:

1. Both the *Magillath Ta'anith* (an ancient Jewish scroll contemporary with Jesus) and the *Judaeos* (circa A.D. 8) indicate Herod died on January 14, 1 B.C.

2. Tertullian (A.D. 160) indicates that Caesar Augustus died 15 years after the birth of Jesus (and began ruling 41 years prior to His birth). Thus the death of Augustus on August 19, A.D. 14 would place the birth of Jesus in 2 B.C.*

3. Irenaeus indicates Jesus was born in the forty-first year of the reign of Augustus (see above).

4. The "father of church history," Eusebius (A.D. 265–340) seems to agree with the above references to Augustus and also ties the birth of Jesus to the deaths of Antony and Cleopatra, further confirming 2 B.C.

5. If we work backward from the beginning of the ministry of Jesus and John the Baptist, an estimate of 2 B.C. seems most likely. We know the ministries began in the fifteenth year of the reign of Tiberius Caesar, which history pinpoints as A.D. 29 (Luke 3:1). Jewish law required men to be 30 years of age before starting ministry; and Luke indicates Jesus was "about 30 years old" (Luke 3:23). Working backward would place the birth in 2 B.C.

*Note: There is no "year zero," which must be taken into account in calculations.

Was Jesus Just a Man?

For some people, accepting the eyewitness testimony may lead to still more questions. The accounts don't merely indicate that a great man named Jesus was born. They indicate that God came to earth in human flesh. That Jesus was born of a virgin—having been conceived by God's Holy Spirit. They indicate Jesus performed miracles which helped prove He was the Son of God—and that He became the Savior of the world when He rose from the dead after a violent crucifixion. How do we know Jesus was not just a "good teacher" or "prophet"? Some compelling reasons are:

1. Those who knew the truth died violent deaths to prove it.[9]

The people who were with Jesus constantly during his ministry, the disciples, knew for a fact whether Jesus had proven Himself to be God by overcoming death. According to tradition, all but John died a violent death rather than renounce the gospel.

Peter—*crucified upside down*	**Bartholomew**—*crucified*
James* (Jesus' brother)—*stoned*	**Andrew**—*crucified*
Matthew—*death by sword*	**Philip**—*crucified*
James, son of Alphaeus—*crucified*	**Simon**—*crucified*
James, son of Zebedee—*death by sword*	**Thomas**—*speared*
Thaddaeus—*killed by arrows*	**Paul***—*beheaded*
John—*natural death*	

*Came to believe after the resurrection

Martyrdom for a *cause* is not unusual. But martyrdom for a *lie—when the truth is known*—makes no sense. The disciples knew of Jesus' claim to be God. They knew of His promise to overcome death. They saw Him die. They were in a position to *know* for certain if His resurrection was real. Why would anyone—let alone 12 people—die for a God that was a *fake?*

2. Millions chose death over renouncing Jesus.

Underneath Rome lie 900 miles of carved caves—the Catacombs—where more than seven million Christians were buried. Many of these graves those people who chose execution by horrible means rather than renounce Jesus. Early Christians hiding in the Catacombs would certainly have spoken directly with eyewitnesses of Jesus. After about A.D. 400, the Catacombs were buried and forgotten for more than 1000 years. In 1578 they were rediscovered by accident. Today they can be seen as silent memorials to the many who died rather than curse Jesus or bow down to an emperor's statue.

Was Jesus Just a "Great Prophet"?

Some nonbelieving Jews and others say that Jesus was a "great prophet," but not the Messiah and not the Son of God.

Such a statement is self-contradictory. A prophet by definition had to be 100-percent accurate. Jesus gave prophecy indicating that He was both the Messiah and the Son of God. So if Jesus was a great prophet, He also had to be the Messiah and the Son of God. Otherwise, He was not a prophet.

Considering Jesus' track record on other easily verified prophecies, we would be wise to also believe His most significant claims (see page 42).

3. Paul, one of the greatest persecutors of Christians, changed radically upon seeing the risen Christ.

Hostile testimony from people representing an opposing viewpoint is often the most compelling. Paul, a *leader of the effort to execute Christians,* gave up wealth, prestige, and power to spread the gospel after encountering the risen Christ. Paul went from being a prominent Pharisee to being poverty-stricken, tortured, stoned, shipwrecked, and eventually beheaded (Acts 22; 2 Corinthians 11:23-27). His efforts resulted in the writing of much of the New Testament and the start of many early Christian churches.

4. Prophecies written hundreds of years before Jesus identify Him specifically.

Prophecies with details about the "who," "what," "when," and "where" of Jesus were recorded centuries before the first Christmas. We have in existence today ancient manuscripts of hundreds of precise prophecies (see pages 20–23).

How Do We Know the Records Are Accurate?

Scribes

The position of a Jewish scribe was one of the most demanding and esteemed positions of Biblical times. Scribes were trained for years and were permitted to practice the profession only after age 30. They were sometimes referred to as doctors of the law, and they joined the priests in helping others understand the Jewish law.

Scriptural Copy Rules[1]

Recording of holy Scripture was a serious responsibility. So important was its exact reproduction that Jewish scribes were forced to adhere to these demanding rules any time a manuscript was copied:

1. *Scrolls*—special paper, ink, and surface preparation were required.

2. *Tight specifications*—number of columns, 37 letters per column.

3. *Master used*—no duplicates of duplicates.

4. *Each letter*—visually confirmed. No writing of phrases.

5. *Distance between letters*—checked with a thread.

6. *Alphabet*—each letter counted and compared to the original.

7. *Letters per page*—all were counted and compared to the master.

8. *Middle letter of scroll*—verified to be same as on the master.

9. *One mistake*—the scroll was destroyed if it was intended to be a master.

The Dead Sea Scrolls

Any doubt regarding the accurate transmission of the manuscripts was erased in 1947 with the discovery of hundreds of scrolls buried for nearly 2000 years. Many were written more than 100 years before Christ. Comparison with recent Jewish copies shows virtually no change.

Was Jesus God?

Christians claim that Jesus was in reality God appearing to the world in human flesh. The Christian concept of the one God of the universe includes three distinctly different, yet inextricable parts (or "persons"): the Father, the Son (Jesus), and the Holy Spirit. Though this is difficult to understand, analogies have been made to H_2O, which can exist as water, ice, and vapor; and to light, which has the physical properties of both waves and particles.

Did Jesus Think He Was God?

Many times Jesus referred to His own deity, both directly and indirectly. Although Jesus confirmed that He was the Messiah (Mark 14:61,63), He did not use the term "Messiah" to refer to Himself—perhaps to differentiate Him in His deity from the widespread expectation of a *human* Messiah. Jesus often used the terms "Son of Man" and "Son of God" of Himself. Both referred to His divine nature (Daniel 7:13,14; Matthew 26:63,64). Jesus also used the specific words "I am" (*Ego eimi* in Greek, *ani bu* in Hebrew) on several occasions (for example, in John 8:56-58). These are the same words God used to describe Himself to Moses. Jesus also stated specifically that He and God "are one" (John 10:30).

And Jesus clearly indicated He had authority over matters controlled only by God, such as forgiveness of sin (Mark 2:5-10). Also divine were the timeless power of His words (Matthew 24:35) and His glory (John 17:5). Significant also was Jesus' acceptance of worship (Luke 5:8; John 20:28). The intensely monotheistic foundation of the Jews would absolutely forbid any worship of anything but the one true God. Analysis of Jesus' life—His compassionate miracles, His perfect lifestyle, and His love—support his claims, providing additional evidence of His divinity.

Did Others Think of Jesus as God?

The disciples came to view Jesus as God in human flesh, and they worshiped Him as such (Luke 5:8; John 20:28). Their witnessing of the resurrection and the transfiguration (Matthew 17:18) provided them with strong evidence. The New Testament and early Christian writings define Jesus to be God—*our Lord*—here on earth (1 Corinthians 8:6; 1 Timothy 2:5).

Is There Other Evidence of Jesus' Deity?

Many say Jesus' miracles are evidence of His deity. But there are records of miracles that were performed by others (in the Bible and elsewhere). The Bible states that perfect fulfillment of prophecy proves God's intervention (Deuteronomy 18:21, 22). The odds of all Old Testament prophecies about Jesus coming true in *any one man* are beyond statistical possibility without divine intervention (see pages 20–23). Jesus prophesied with *perfect* accuracy about such things as the precise timing of His death, the exact manner of His death, His resurrection, and His later appearance in Galilee. His prophetic perfection taken together with His claim to be God verifies Jesus' deity.

Common Questions

The Star—What Was It?

Many planetariums acknowledge the occurrence of a conjunction of Jupiter and Saturn in the constellation of "The Fishes" in 7 B.C. Clay tablets found in Babylonia, which were written in the previous year, indicate the magi were looking forward to the event as one of great significance. Symbolically, Jupiter represented a world ruler. Saturn was regarded as the "star" of Palestine, and "The Fishes" represented the "last days." This knowledge, combined with the biblical prophecies which Daniel would certainly have taught the magi, may have initiated the magi's journey to see Jesus. Even other prophecy not contained in the Bible may have prompted this journey. However, there are many other possible explanations of the "star of Bethlehem," including the possibility of a nova (a star that suddenly increases in brightness).

The magi's final guide to the location of Jesus (Matthew 2:9) was more likely a different manifestation of God's glory, sometimes referred to as the *shekinah* glory. Other examples of *shekinah* glory in the Bible are the cloud of the exodus (Exodus 13:21) and the glory that shone on the shepherds (Luke 2:9).

What Was the Meaning of the Gifts of the Magi?

Gold, frankincense, and myrrh were significant gifts, given in consideration of the role of Jesus in the world. Gold, the most precious metal at that time, was the symbol of royalty. Frankincense was an expensive fragrance which played a special role in worship (Leviticus 2:2). And myrrh was an embalming substance (a surprising gift for a newborn baby). Together these gifts describe Jesus as a Savior for the world (myrrh—for His death as a blood sacrifice), who would receive ultimate ruling authority (gold—for His kingship) and worship (frankincense— for His deity).

Do We Know the Actual Date of Christmas?

The first Christmas probably occurred in the spring or summer— a more likely time for shepherds to be in the fields (sheep were almost never taken out after October). The ancient pagan holidays of the *Saturnalia* traditionally began on December 19 and were characterized by feasting, gift-giving, special music, lighting of candles, green trees, and great revelry. As Christianity spread, these holidays were given Christian connotations. The official Roman holiday of Christmas was decreed by Emperor Constantine in A.D. 336. However, because of its pagan origin, Christmas was actually outlawed in England in the 1600s and was banned in some areas until recently.

Why Do Some People Reject Jesus?

With the wealth of evidence we have available, it seems incredible that some people (including many Jews) reject Jesus as the Messiah. This, however, was clearly prophesied (Isaiah 53:1-3; Psalm 118:22; Matthew 21:42-46; Luke 16:19-31). We also need to realize that many people *do* accept Jesus as the Messiah (including Jews). Virtually all of the first Christians were Jews, and Christianity wasn't officially separated from Judaism until it began to threaten the Jewish leaders of that time. Some scholars estimate that about 70 percent of Jerusalem's population was Christian when the city was conquered in A.D. 70.

What If I Don't Believe the Entire Bible?

Having a relationship with God does not depend on your believing the entire Bible. Belief in Jesus as Savior and asking Him to be director of your life are all that is required. Some people wonder why God uses prophecy and sometimes uses cryptic wording. There is no absolute answer to this. Perhaps God wants people to seek Him and then find Him. Perhaps He wants to emphasize the need for faith. Or perhaps He wants to allow the Holy Spirit to reach different people in different ways. Even so, general and obvious evidence for the reliability of the Bible is also abundant for everyone.

How Can We Ensure the Right Relationship So We Can Go to Heaven?

When Jesus said not all who use His name will enter heaven (Matthew 7:21-23), He was referring to people who think using Christ's name along with rituals and rules is the key to heaven. A relationship with God is *not* based on rituals and rules. It's based on grace and forgiveness, and on the right kind of relationship with Him.

How to Have a Personal Relationship with God

1. Believe that God exists and that He came to earth in the human form of Jesus Christ (John 3:16; Romans 10:9).

2. Accept God's free forgiveness of sins through the death and resurrection of Jesus Christ (Ephesians 2:8-10; 1:7,8).

3. Switch to God's plan for life (1 Peter 1:21-23; Ephesians 2:1-5).

4. Express desire for Christ to be director of your life (Matthew 7:21-27; 1 John 4:15).

Prayer for Eternal Life with God

"Dear God, I believe You sent Your Son, Jesus, to die for my sins so I can be forgiven. I'm sorry for my sins, and I want to live the rest of my life the way You want me to. Please put Your Spirit in my life to direct me. Amen."

Then What?

People who have sincerely taken these steps automatically become members of God's family of believers. A new world of freedom and strength is available through prayer and obedience to God's will. New believers can build their relationship with God by taking the following steps:

- Find a Bible-based church that you like and attend regularly.
- Try to set aside some time each day to pray and read the Bible.
- Locate other Christians to spend time with on a regular basis.

God's Promises to Believers

For Today

But seek first His kingdom and His righteousness,
and all these things [things to satisfy all your needs]
will be given to you as well.
—Matthew 6:33

For Eternity

Whoever believes in the Son has eternal life,
but whoever rejects the Son will not see life,
for God's wrath remains on him.
—John 3:36

Once we develop an eternal perspective, even the greatest problems on earth fade in significance.

Notes

1. Mc Dowell, Josh, and Wilson, Bill, *A Ready Defense*. San Bernardino, CA: Here's Life Publishers, Inc., 1990.

2. McRay, John, *Archaeology & the New Testament*. Grand Rapids, MI: Baker Book House, 1991.

3. Green, Michael, *Who Is This Jesus?* Nashville, TN: Thomas Nelson, 1992.

4. *Encyclopedia Britannica*. Chicago, IL: 1993.

5. Rosen, Moishe, *Y'shua*. Chicago, IL: Moody Bible Institute, 1982.

6. Missler, Chuck, *Footprints of the Messiah*, audiotape. Coeur d'Alene, ID: Koinonia House Inc., 1995.

7. Missler, Chuck, *Romance of Redemption*, audiotape. Coeur d'Alene, ID: Koinonia House Inc., 1995.

8. Missler, Chuck, *Christmas Story*, audiotape. Coeur d'Alene, ID: Koinonia House Inc., 1995.

9. MacArthur, John F. Jr., *God with Us*. Grand Rapids, MI: Zondervan Publishing House, 1989.

Bibliography

Free, Joseph P., and Vos, Howard F., *Archeology and Bible History*. Grand Rapids, MI: Zondervan, 1969.

Freeman, James M., *Manners and Customs of the Bible*. Plainfield, NJ: LOGOS International, 1972.

Hirshberg & Simon, "The First Christmas," *Life* Magazine. New York, NY: December 1992.

Josephus, Flavius, translated by Whiston, Wm., *The Complete Works of Josephus*. Grand Rapids, MI: Kregel, 1981.

Keely, Robin, *Jesus 2000*. Batavia, IL: Lion Publishing, 1989.

McDowell, Josh, and Wilson, Bill, *He Walked Among Us*. Nashville, TN: Thomas Nelson, Inc., 1993.

Muncaster, Ralph O., *The Bible—General Analysis—Investigation of the Evidence*. Mission Viejo, CA: Strong Basis to Believe, 1996.

Muncaster, Ralph O., *Jesus—Investigation of the Evidence*. Mission Viejo, CA: Strong Basis to Believe, 1996.

Readers Digest, *ABC's of the Bible*. Pleasantville, NY, 1991.

Readers Digest, *Who's Who in the Bible*. Pleasantville, NY, 1994.

Ross, Hugh, Ph.D., *The Fingerprint of God*. Orange, CA: Promise Publishing Co., 1989.

Shanks, Hershel (editor), *Understanding the Dead Sea Scrolls*. New York, NY: Vintage Books, 1993.

Smith, F. LaGard, *The Daily Bible in Chronological Order*. Eugene, OR: Harvest House, 1984.

Walvoord, John F., *The Prophecy Knowledge Handbook*. Wheaton, IL: Victor Books, 1984.

Youngblood, Ronald F., *New Illustrated Bible Dictionary*. Nashville, TN: Nelson, 1995.